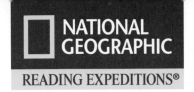

PLANET PROTECTORS

The Energy Stars

CLEAN, SAFE HYDROGEN

By Barbara Keeler

Illustrated by Barbara Kiwak

PICTURE CREDITS
3-7 (top left), 3 (top right), 4 (top right), 6 (top right), 60 (top right), 60-64 (top left), 62 (top right), 64 (top right) Corbis; 5 (top right), 7 (top right), 61 (top right), 63 (top right) Getty Images; 4 © AP Photo/Ahn Young-joon; 5 © AP Photo/Bill Haber; 60 © Sean Sprague/The Image Works; 61 © Alex Farnsworth/The Image Works; 62 © Chris Windsor/Photodisc/Getty Images; 64 © BIOS/Peter Arnold, Inc.

PUBLISHED BY THE NATIONAL GEOGRAPHIC SOCIETY
Produced through the worldwide resources of the National Geographic Society, John M. Fahey, Jr., President and Chief Executive Officer; Gilbert M. Grosvenor, Chairman of the Board.

PREPARED BY NATIONAL GEOGRAPHIC SCHOOL PUBLISHING
Sheron Long, Chief Executive Officer; Samuel Gesumaria, President; Francis Downey, Vice President and Publisher; Richard Easby, Editorial Manager; Anne M. Stone, Editor; Margaret Sidlosky, Director of Design and Illustrations; Jim Hiscott, Design Manager; Cynthia Olson, Ruth Ann Thompson, Art Directors; Matt Wascavage, Director of Publishing Services; Lisa Pergolizzi, Production Manager.

MANUFACTURING AND QUALITY CONTROL
Christopher A. Liedel, Chief Financial Officer; Phillip L. Schlosser, Vice President; Clifton M. Brown III, Director.

CONSULTANTS
Mary Anne Wengel and Gretchen Wieman

BOOK DESIGN
Steve Curtis Design, Inc.

Published by the National Geographic Society
1145 17th Street N.W.
Washington, D.C. 20036-4688

Product #4U1005113
ISBN: 978-1-4263-5106-8

Printed in Mexico.

12
10 9 8 7 6 5 4 3 2

TABLE OF CONTENTS

The Setting 4

The Characters 6

Chapter 1   An Energy Crisis 9

Chapter 2   Saving Energy 23

Chapter 3   The Class Seeks Answers 31

Chapter 4   The Town Climbs Aboard 48

The Facts Behind the Story 60

Read, Research, and Write 63

Extend Your Reading 64

How We Use Energy

Think about all the ways people use energy. Lighting and heating your house takes energy. Cooking food takes energy. So does watching television, using a computer, or playing music.

When you get on a bus to go to school, that bus needs energy to run. Your school uses energy to light classrooms and cook lunch. People use vast amounts of energy every day. In fact, energy is such a big part of people's lives that it is easy to take it for granted. As the world's population grows, the need for more energy grows. People are looking for ways to supply everyone with the energy they need. They are also looking for ways to use less energy.

Oil rig

Where We Get Energy

People get energy from many sources. However, burning fossil fuels is our main energy source. Fossil fuels include coal, oil, and natural gas. Burning fossil fuels produces most of the electricity in the United States. Nearly all vehicles run on gasoline. Gasoline is made from oil.

Burning fossil fuels creates pollution. The supply of fossil fuel is not endless. One day supplies will run out. Scientists are learning to reduce pollution from fossil fuels. They are coming up with ways to make fossil fuels last longer.

Many people think it is important to use fewer fossil fuels. Scientists are researching other energy sources. New energy sources may be cleaner and may not run out.

Meet the Characters

Dr. Nelson

Jack's dad is known as the town's nutty professor. He is a scientist at a local university. He studies ways to save energy.

Jack

Jack Nelson is a sixth-grade student who lives in Vermont. His house is run using energy from the sun, wind, and especially hydrogen. He is teased because his family's lifestyle is different.

Mr. Schmidt

The Schmidts own the town's gas stations. They also supply heating oil.

Carlos

Carlos is Jack's best friend. His mother is a vice president at the power plant. She gets blamed when the plant cannot supply enough electricity.

Gretchen

Gretchen is Jack's classmate. She is the captain of the soccer team and the best player. She is kind, but nobody messes with her.

Gary

Gary Schmidt also plays soccer on the school team. He does not like Jack and gives him a hard time.

CHAPTER 1

An Energy Crisis

From his yard on the mountaintop, Jack could see for miles. Fall had arrived early this year and Jack looked out over the colorful leaves. The forest that covered the mountain was splashed with green, gold, orange, and red.

The flatland at the bottom of the mountain had been cleared for farmland and a small town. The fields, farms, and orchards stretched as far as Jack could see. A river cut through the town and flowed past the farms and fields.

Jack's eyes followed the road that wound its way down the mountain. It continued to the town and the school. Jack could make out the green soccer field where he would practice later. The road continued past the farms.

"Quite a view," said Mr. Block.

"It is," said Jack. "But that's not the only reason we live here. We live here so we can get as much sun and wind as possible."

Mr. Block was a builder. He had come to see Jack's house. Scientists, builders, and many other people came from all over the country to see Jack's house.

Jack's father, Dr. Nelson was a scientist and a professor at a university a few miles away. He specialized in energy **conservation** and using different sources of energy. Everything in Jack's house was powered by a gas called hydrogen. Even the family car ran on hydrogen.

Jack had helped his parents build the house. He was proud when people came to learn from his dad's work. On the other hand, he was tired of being teased at school. Many people in town didn't take his dad's work seriously. They sometimes called him the nutty professor.

Mr. Block was interested in Dad's work, though. He listened as Jack explained, "On the mountaintop, we're above the clouds and fog on some days. There's nothing to cast shadows in the early morning or evening. We usually get more sun than we would down near town."

"Not much sun today," said Mr. Block.

"That's true, so today we're using wind power to make electricity." Jack pointed to the spinning blades of a wind machine. The blades turned at the top of a pole. The pole extended from the roof of a building behind the garage. "We use the electricity we make from the

conservation – the protection of natural resources, such as soil, water, or forests

wind or sun to change water into hydrogen and oxygen. Water is made of hydrogen and oxygen. Electricity runs a machine that takes water and then separates the hydrogen from the oxygen."

"The wind is blowing hard today." said Mr. Block. "Your wind machine must be making a lot of electricity. Can you store any electricity you don't use, Dr. Nelson?"

"Yes we can. When we're finished making the hydrogen we need, we store the remaining electricity in batteries."

"Hydrogen does seem to have possibilities. I'd sure like to get a hydrogen heater to test it out," said Block. "I don't know if I'll be able to get enough heating oil this winter. Even if I can, the price will be sky-high. Will I need a high-tech set up like this to use hydrogen?"

"Your best bet is hydrogen fuel cells," said Dad. "I have a friend in the California desert who makes them. He uses solar power from sunlight to make electricity. He gets sun, year-round, so he can make a lot of electricity. That allows him to make a lot of hydrogen. Other companies are making the fuel cells too. I have some catalogs in the house you can have."

Block was impressed with the electrolyzer that made the hydrogen. He was also impressed with the appliances that ran on hydrogen. The house did not use much hydrogen though. It was designed to use energy efficiently.

"I really like what I see. But I don't know how well houses with renewable energy will sell," said Block. "We have an oil shortage right now. But I'm afraid that I'll build these houses and finish them just when it's easy to get oil again. If people can get all the oil and electricity they want, they might not want to buy houses that use hydrogen and have wind machines."

"People have to realize that we have an energy crisis whether or not we can get oil today and tomorrow," said Dad. "Earth has only so much oil, gas, and coal. Every year we use more. Someday these **fossil fuels** will all be used up."

"Besides," said Jack, "We make pollution and tear up the land when we use oil, coal, and gas. We cause oil spills, explosions, and accidents in mines."

"I agree. Pollution is a growing problem. You say burning hydrogen doesn't make any air pollution? Not even carbon dioxide?" asked Block.

"No," said Dad. "Unlike fossil fuels, hydrogen doesn't contain carbon. Burning carbon produces carbon dioxide. This gas is making global warming worse."

"Another kudo for hydrogen. We sure don't need any more greenhouse gases," Block thought for a minute. "If the price of fossil fuels goes way up, people will probably

---

fossil fuels – A fuel formed from the remains of plants and animals that died long ago. Coal and oil are fossil fuels

want houses that are more energy efficient. They may want to buy houses that run on renewable energy like yours."

"You got it!" said Dad. "One reason that people don't develop more energy from wind, sun, hydrogen, and other renewable methods is that fossil fuels are cheap. If fossil fuels were more expensive, people would start saving energy and using more sources of renewable energy."

The phone rang. Jack picked it up. It was Carlos. "How come you haven't answered any of my emails today?" asked Jack.

"I can't turn on the computer," said Carlos. "We have no electricity. Didn't you know we're having a blackout?"

"How would I know?" asked Jack. "We make our own electricity. Remember?"

"Right! Can your dad take me to soccer practice?" said Carlos. "Mom hasn't been able to buy enough gas to drive to work during the week. She doesn't want to use gas driving me around. I wish we had more bike paths. Mom won't let me ride my bike on the road into town."

"Yes, we'll pick you up," said Jack.

Dad said goodbye to Mr. Block and disappeared into the garage. A few minutes later the garage door opened and he backed into the driveway. He was driving a blue minivan. It looked like any other, but the engine was very different. This car ran on hydrogen. Instead of using gasoline it had hydrogen fuel cells.

Jack opened the door, climbed into the passenger seat, and fastened his seat belt. Dad started the engine. They bumped slowly down the unpaved driveway to the road.

The drive to school was about ten miles. The road snaked around and down the mountain. They wound through trees of bright red, yellow, and orange leaves.

On the way they stopped to pick up three other players who lived on the mountain. Ride sharing was becoming more common as people looked for ways to save gas. The first player they picked up was May. The second was Gretchen, the captain of the team and the best player.

The middle school was small. It didn't have enough soccer players for both a boys' team and a girls' team. Instead, the boys and girls played on the same team. Most of the other schools they played against were also small. Some of them also had mixed teams.

Dad picked Carlos up last. "This electricity blackout is affecting a lot of the power plant's customers," said Carlos. His mother was a vice president at the power plant that supplied electricity to the town and other small towns in Vermont. "The plant still burns oil to make electricity. Like everyone else, the plant can only get so much oil. Mom says part of the problem is that since people are having trouble getting heating oil, they bought electric heaters. Electric heaters use a lot of electricity. And the plant doesn't have extra oil to make extra electricity."

The sun came out as Dad drove down the mountain. "What's that line of cars up ahead?" asked Jack.

"You got me!" said Dad. "We never have traffic jams on this road."

Ahead, a line of cars was stopped dead. Jack got out and walked up to the car in front. The driver rolled down the window. "What's going on?" asked Jack.

"Beats me!" said the driver. "I'm just trying to get to town. The line creeps forward every five minutes or so."

Jack jogged back to the car. Dad rolled the window down. "I'll go up to the front of the line, and see what's going on," said Jack.

"Thanks," said Dad. "If we start moving, we'll pick you up when we catch up."

Jack ran beside the road, breathing in the crisp autumn air. Dry leaves crunched under his feet as he ran. He noticed there were no cars coming from the other direction.

Jack was a good runner. In college, his dad had set records in long-distance running. Jack hoped to follow in his footsteps.

Before long Jack reached the head of the line of cars. The line turned into Schmidt's gas station. Cars were also lined up from the opposite direction.

Jack ran back to the car. He opened the door. "It's a gas line!" he said. "Some of the cars are just waiting to get by. A lot of them are waiting for gas. It's safe for us to drive on the wrong side of the road. No cars can get through from the opposite direction. When we pass the gas station, you can get back on this side of the road."

"Have people turned their engines off?" asked Dad.

"Most of them are running," said Jack.

Dad's face turned red. "That's a waste of gas! It takes more gas to idle an engine for one minute than to start it up again! If people shut off their engines they'd save gas."

Jack glanced in the backseat. Gretchen and May were grinning at each other. When they saw Jack looking, they pulled the corners of their mouths in and looked out of the window. Jack climbed into the front seat.

Carlos cleared his throat, breaking the awkward silence. "I guess all these cars just sitting with their engines running are using gas to wait to buy gas. That leaves less gas for the rest of us."

"You know, that's right!" said Gretchen.

Dad couldn't leave it at that. "And every time we waste gas or heating oil, we're wasting an energy supply that will eventually run out."

Jack knew Dad was right. Even so, he wished Dad wouldn't rant in front of his friends. He was tired of being known as the son of a nutty scientist.

Dad pulled into the empty left lane. He drove slowly and carefully past the line of cars. When they reached the gas station, they read a sign over the pumps: ONLY 3 GALLONS PER CUSTOMER. A red-faced man stood by his car at the pump. He was shaking his fist and yelling at Mr. Schmidt.

Mr. Schmidt and Dad didn't get along. Whenever Dad showed the school or the city how to use less energy, Schmidt opposed him. Even so, Dad said, "The gas limit is not Schmidt's fault. He just doesn't have much gas to sell. He's trying to be fair to as many people as possible."

"The three-gallon limit adds to the gas line problem though," said Gretchen. "Once these people get their three gallons, they'll drive to another gas station and get three gallons there. So all three gas stations in town have lines."

"The car washes too," said Carlos. "The car washes will sell three gallons of gas, but only with a car wash. Mom has to drive all the way to the power plant five times a week. She spends her weekends waiting in line at gas stations and car washes. She needs to fill her tank for her commute during the week. Our car is sure clean though."

"Schmidt gives first priority to the school and city," said Dad. "Nobody gets any gas until the fire trucks, ambulance, and police cars have enough. Then he makes sure the school bus has enough gas. Students on the farms and mountains live as far as fifteen miles away. The buses use a lot of gas picking up and dropping off all the kids."

"I wish they'd use the bus to get us to practice and to games out of town," said May.

"The district didn't want to pay for the drivers or the gas—even when they could get gas," said Dad. "But having all the parents driving uses more gas than one school bus would."

"Mr. Schmidt hasn't delivered any heating oil for a long time either," said Gretchen.

"That's because he doesn't have any. When he has some, he'll deliver it," said Dad. Jack was proud that Dad was so fair. He could stand up for Schmidt even though they didn't like each other.

"It's starting to get cold at night, and it's going to be really cold soon," said May.

Dad followed the road until he came to the turnoff to town. They drove a mile to a grassy field. This field was used for most of the outdoor team sports. At one end of the field was a large sign that said Schmidt Field.

The Schmidts were generous. They donated money to the school and to the city. In fact, they had bought the uniforms for all the sports teams. They expected their donations to buy something though—a lot of control.

The team piled out and Dad drove off. Gretchen asked, "How come your dad never stops for gas? He always gives me rides, but I've never seen him stop for gas."

Jack looked down. Sometimes he felt like a freak.

Carlos answered, "The van runs on hydrogen."

"Awesome!" said Gretchen.

"Too weird!" said a voice from behind.

Jack turned around. The boy who had spoken was standing next to Gary Schmidt. "Hello Hydrogen Head," said Gary. The other boys snickered. Gary always gave Jack a hard time. Mostly he teased him about his father being a nutty scientist.

Jack knew the real reason Gary put him down. The Schmidt family fortune had been built on selling gasoline and oil. They owned all three gas stations in town. They also sold all the heating oil. The Schmidts were threatened by Dad's success with alternative energy. The Schmidts didn't like Jack's parents, and Gary didn't like Jack.

"Don't you ever get tired of being a world-class jerk?" Gary turned and found himself looking into Gretchen's eyes. Gretchen was the only sixth grader who could keep him in line. She was taller and stronger than most of the boys at school. Nobody crossed her, on or off the soccer field. Gary dropped his eyes and walked away.

Gretchen walked over to the coach of the soccer team and they began talking intently. Coach Hu waved to the team and practice began.

In the scrimmage, Gary and Jack were on opposing teams. During the scrimmage, Gary elbowed Jack in the stomach. While Jack was recovering, Gary scored a goal. Breathing heavily, Jack reminded himself not to let Gary get to him. Thinking about their conflicts would only take his mind off the game. It didn't help that Gary fouled him every chance he got.

After the game, Jack, Carlos, Gretchen and May waited for Dad. The team had played hard. The sun was setting and it had gotten colder. Jack hoped his father would arrive soon.

The practice had been very rough. Jack was bruised and scratched.

"I don't think all those fouls were accidental," said Gretchen.

"Seriously?" said Jack. "All against me? What are the odds of that happening?"

Gretchen walked a short distance away. She beckoned for Gary to join her. Jack watched Gretchen talking to Gary angrily. Her hands were on her hips, and her brows drawn together fiercely. Gary held out his hands, palms up. He shook his head, looking innocent.

Jack only could hear bits of what Gretchen was saying: ". . . . not fooling anyone. . . . sportsmanship. . . . "

Dad drove up. Gretchen left Gary and ran over. "Does your car really run on hydrogen, Dr. Nelson?" she asked.

"It sure does! Want to see the engine?"

The whole team crowded around the car, except Gary and his friends. One of his friends started heading toward the car. Gary grabbed his arm and pulled him back. They stood watching from a distance.

Jack chuckled, thinking about how hard it must be for Gary to stay away from the engine. He knew Gary was a

nut about engines. On days when he didn't have a game or practice, he rushed to his father's gas station. There he helped the mechanics repair cars. He wasn't paid, but he never seemed to get tired of it.

As they drove away, Jack saw Gary and his friends clustered around a boy who had seen the engine. They seemed to be questioning him. The boy's hands were moving—probably to show how the engine parts worked.

CHAPTER 2

Saving Energy

I need to stop at the hardware store," said Dad. He parked about a half block from the store. Everyone got out of the car and walked along behind him.

As they passed the laundromat, Jack saw Mrs. Chin inside. She was bundled up in a huge coat and scarf. Huddled next to the dryers, she was sewing a button on a shirt. Beside her was a basket full of clean clothes, already folded.

"Wait," said Jack. "Let's stop and help Mrs. Chin carry her laundry home." He opened the door and went into the laundromat. Everyone followed.

"Hello, Mrs. Chin," said Jack. "May we carry your clothes for you?"

"That's a nice offer," said Mrs. Chin. "But I'm not ready to go back to my cold apartment yet. As I've grown older, I've become very sensitive to cold. It's warm here by the dryers. I'm just going to stay here and finish my sewing. It's hard to sew with cold fingers. I can keep my fingers warm in here."

"Why is your apartment cold?" asked Carlos.

"I'm nearly out of oil. I have only enough left to heat my water. I don't want to use it all up."

"I might be able to help," said Dad, "Will you show me your apartment?"

Jack picked up Mrs. Chin's basket of laundry. They all headed for Ms. Chin's apartment two doors away. The building had two apartments, one above the other. Mrs. Chin lived on the bottom floor.

"The apartment upstairs is always warmer than mine, even without the heater," she said. "The warm air rises."

"That's right. The heat from your apartment goes up into the apartment above you," said Jack.

"Doesn't Mr. Bikakis own this building?" asked Dad.

"Yes," said Mrs. Chin.

"I'll talk to him about putting in a ceiling fan," said Dad. "When you turn it on, it will push some of the rising warm air back down. It should keep your place warmer."

Dad looked around. "Even when you turn on the heat, you're losing a lot of it. Part of your problem is that the heat in the house is escaping outdoors."

He walked over to the window and felt around the window frame. "You have too much space between the windows and their frames."

Dad then looked at the door. "You also have a large space between the bottom of the door and the floor. Tomorrow I'll put up weather strips. For now this will help." He rolled up a towel and put it against the bottom of the door.

Dad examined the windows. "I'll also talk to Mr. Bikakis about putting in some double-glazed windows. They're made with two sheets of glass. The sheets have a layer of gas between them. Heat doesn't move through gas as quickly as it does through glass. The windows will keep the heat inside your house."

"Meanwhile, I'll pick up some plastic window sheeting at the hardware store. I'll put it on your windows. Will any of you kids help?" Everyone nodded.

Jack inspected Mrs. Chin's water heater. "You're losing heat here, too. Dad, shouldn't these pipes and the heater be wrapped in something to keep the heat in?"

"Yes. I'll get some insulation to wrap around your water heater," said Dad. "We'll also wrap it around those pipes. That will keep you from losing so much heat."

"I have an extra heater you can use until you have heating oil," said Dad. "It uses a hydrogen fuel cell. You won't have to use any heating oil or electricity. Keep it in the room where you are. Close the doors to the other rooms so that you don't lose the heat."

"That's very nice of you. I didn't know that hydrogen could run a heater. Is it safe?" asked Mrs. Chin

"Any heater needs to be handled with care, but fuel cells are very safe," said Dad.

He then checked the filters and the vent of the oil heater. "These vents and the filter are dirty. That means the heater needs to work harder. It takes more heating oil to heat your apartment. The kids can help me clean them for you tomorrow."

"I can do that myself," said Mrs. Chin. "One thing I do really well is clean!"

Jack said, "If you keep your drapes open during the day the sunlight coming through the window will heat the rooms inside. Then, when the sun sets, or stops shining through your window, close the drapes to keep the heat in."

Dad looked at Mrs. Chin's windows. "Are these thin curtains all you have? You don't seem to have any window shades or blinds either."

"These curtains are all I've ever had," said Mrs. Chin.

"I'll also talk to Mr. Bikakis about putting in some window shades and heavy drapes," said Dad. "For tonight, I'll hang some blankets or towels over the windows. That will stop some of the heat from escaping."

As they went out the door, Jack said, "Don't forget to put the towel back against the bottom of the door."

"Thank you for all the ideas and the help," said Mrs. Chin.

After they left the hardware store they stopped at Hank's Food Mart for some cold drinks. Gretchen opened the door to the cold case.

"Gretchen, look at the products through the glass. Decide what you want before you open the door," said

Dad. "If you stand and look with the door open, you
waste a lot of energy."

Jack looked at the ceiling. He wished he could sink
through the floor. His dad was lecturing again.

Gretchen surprised Jack though. "Oops, sorry. You're
right," she said. "Too bad we can't see through our
refrigerator doors at home."

Carlos pointed to some open coolers with no doors.
"Mom says these waste a lot of electricity. They end up
cooling the whole store. It makes customers cold and it
uses more electricity to keep the food cold."

"Thank you!" said Dad in a booming voice. Jack rolled his eyes. "I've been talking to Hank about that for years. Maybe if your Mom talked to him he'd listen. She could tell him how much money he could save by keeping things in closed refrigerators."

"Don't you ever get tired of yourself?" said a voice behind Jack. He turned and saw Mr. Schmidt holding a bag.

"Selling any hydrogen?" asked Schmidt with a smirk.

"Will you be selling any heating oil?" asked Dad.

Schmidt scowled and his face turned red. "I'll have some before it gets cold."

"People are cold now," said Dad. "What's wrong with having some alternatives when you can't get heating oil? Or when you don't have enough gas to go around?"

"We just need to drill for more oil," said Schmidt. "There's still plenty of oil in the ground."

"Earth's oil won't last forever," said Dad.

"Neither will we!" said Schmidt. He stalked off.

As they drove home, Carlos said, "Mom says the electric generating plant is going to send out some tips about saving electricity at home. The tips will come with the next bills. Some will be the same ones you gave to Mrs. Chin."

As Gretchen got out of the car at her house, she said, "Dr. Nelson, you have some good ideas."

After dinner the phone rang. It was Carlos. "I think we may move away," he said glumly.

"Seriously?! But your mother grew up in Vermont!" said Jack.

"Yeah, and she loves it here. But she's tired of the energy problems. People blame the power plant, and her office gets like a war zone. People don't understand that Mom has no control over the blackouts. They blame her. We even get crank calls in the middle of the night."

"I guess crank calls are a good reason to move away," said Jack.

"Papa wants to move to San Francisco, where he grew up. His family is there. He says the climate is so mild that people don't need air-conditioning in the summer. It takes very little energy to keep the house warm in the winter. It's by the ocean, and the ocean keeps the land from getting too hot or too cold. Even better, you can get around on public transportation. You don't need a car. No more gas lines."

"We will all miss you!" said Jack.

"Thanks!" said Carlos. "And I won't know anyone at all in San Francisco!"

Jack was upset for the rest of the evening. Carlos was his best friend. He was the only friend who had ever been to Jack's house. It was hard to imagine life without him.

CHAPTER 3

The Class Seeks Answers

Monday morning Jack, Carlos, Gretchen, and May got off the school bus into a cloud of fumes. They called the old bus Smellow Yellow.

Gary was hanging around with some friends. As Jack got off the bus, Gary said, "If it isn't No Gas Nelson."

"And here we have Gas Line Gary!" said Carlos.

"At least my father has something that people want!" said Gary. "Nobody wants Dr. Nelson's hydrogen."

"Yeah, your father's seen to that!" said Jack. "Hydrogen may solve many of the energy problems we have now, like gas lines. Also, people are cold and can't get heating oil. We need to develop new energy sources . . ." Jack stopped and reddened. He was sounding like his father.

"This is me, caring!" said Gary. He screwed up his face and pretended to brush away tears.

"Too bad cars can't run on hot air," said Gretchen. "Your dad could hook you up to his pump. We'd have enough hot air for all the cars in town." She crossed her arms and looked Gary up and down. He turned on his heel and stalked off. His friends followed.

At the beginning of science class, Ms. Moreno said, "Let's talk about energy. How many of you saw a gas line on the way to school today?"

Most of the kids raised a hand.

"How many of your parents have enough gas to drive to work this week?"

About ten kids raised a hand.

"How many of you have enough heating oil to stay warm at night?"

About five kids raised a hand.

"What are some things we can do to save energy?"

Jack raised his hand. "Parents use a lot of gas driving kids to school activities. They use even more driving them to games that are out of town. If we used the school bus, it would cost the school more. On the other hand, it would save a lot of gas overall."

"Good idea. I'll suggest it as an energy saving measure at the school board meeting tonight," said Ms. Moreno.

"It would be nice if we had some public transportation," said May.

"Most small towns don't have it," said Ms. Moreno.

The class discussed ways to save gas, such as walking, biking, and ride sharing. Carlos said that people would ride bikes more if the town had bike paths beside the roads.

"Another good idea!" said Ms. Moreno. "Maybe at the next town meeting, we should suggest that the town put in bike paths."

"We could save a lot of energy if more people worked at home," said Jack. "My Mom works for the town. She works at home three days a week. So she only has to drive to work two days a week."

Carlos raised his hand. "My mom gave me copies of some tips the power plant is going to send out. They list ways to save electricity. May I pass them out?"

"Yes, please," said Ms. Moreno.

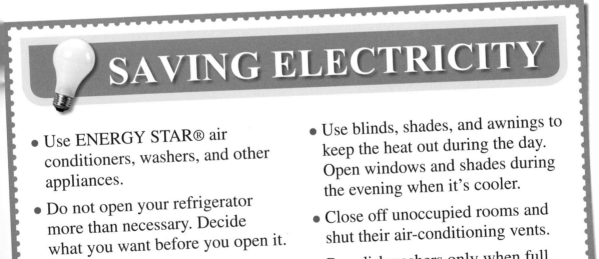

SAVING ELECTRICITY

- Use ENERGY STAR® air conditioners, washers, and other appliances.

- Do not open your refrigerator more than necessary. Decide what you want before you open it.

- Do not set your air conditioner too low. Turn off air-conditioning 30 minutes before you leave your home or office.

- Use blinds, shades, and awnings to keep the heat out during the day. Open windows and shades during the evening when it's cooler.

- Close off unoccupied rooms and shut their air-conditioning vents.

- Run dishwashers only when full. Use the short or economy cycle.

Gretchen helped Carlos pass out the lists.

"How many of your parents bought an electric heater in the last few weeks?" asked Carlos. Fifteen hands went up.

"That solves one problem." said Carlos. "It solves the problem of keeping warm without heating oil. But Ms. Moreno has taught us that some solutions cause new problems. Electric heaters use a lot of energy. If a lot of people start using them all at once, then we may use too much electricity. The power plant may not be able to supply all the electricity we need."

"We need solutions to the whole energy crisis—not just staying warm or gassing our cars," said Ms. Moreno. "One way is to conserve energy. That means to find ways to use less oil, gas, and electricity"

Gretchen raised her hand. "This weekend Dr. Nelson showed us some ways to save heating oil." She told the class about visiting Mrs. Chin. She told them about all of Jack's father's advice to Mrs. Chin.

"These are all steps that we can take now to use less energy," said Ms. Moreno. "But someday people are going to need new sources of energy too. Let's discuss some sources of energy besides fossil fuels."

Different students suggested energy from sun, wind, and moving water. One student had seen a power plant that used heat from inside the earth.

Jack raised his hand. "These are all good sources, but they all have limits. They all affect the environment. To use water power, we usually need to dam up a river and flood valleys. Wind farms use a lot of land, and so do solar farms. It takes a lot of windmills or solar towers to make as much electricity as a fossil fuel plant."

"But you can sometimes use the land for other things," said Gretchen. "For example, wind farms can sometimes have animals grazing among the windmills."

"Do you know of a better energy source, Jack?" asked Ms. Moreno.

"Yes, hydrogen. It is the most plentiful element on Earth," said Jack. "You can make it from water. Burning hydrogen for energy doesn't pollute the air or cause global warming. Neither does using hydrogen fuel cells."

Gary started shaking his head in disgust. Then he put his head down on the desk.

"Jack, tell them about your father's car," said Carlos.

Jack blushed. "It runs on hydrogen. So do a lot of the things in my house."

"Where do you get the hydrogen?" asked Gretchen.

"We make it out of water," said Jack.

"Doesn't making hydrogen take a lot of electricity?" asked Ms. Moreno.

"Yes it does, but we make the electricity from wind and solar power."

"You don't use as much energy as most people, do you?" asked Carlos.

"No," said Jack. "Our house is designed to use as little energy as possible, no matter what source we use."

"I think a field trip would help us understand energy use," said Ms. Moreno. "We could go to Jack's house. It could be a science lesson. We might even get some ideas about how to save energy at school."

Everyone except Gary was nodding. Gary was rolling his eyes while Ms. Moreno's eyes were on Jack.

"Will you ask your father's permission Jack? I'll also write a note."

"Sure," said Jack. "I'm sure he'll be happy to hear we want to visit. Dad has scientists and builders visiting all the time. He's been trying to get people from this town to visit for years. He wants the town to use some of his ideas. Nobody's wanted to visit until now."

"Nobody in this town was stupid enough!" said Gary.

Ms. Moreno stared at him through narrowed eyes. "We'll talk!" she said sternly. Gary looked at the floor.

After class, Ms. Moreno kept Gary behind. Jack could not see Gary's face, but he could see Ms. Moreno's. Jack was glad he wasn't in Gary's shoes.

That afternoon, Coach Hu asked, "Where's Gary? He's late!"

"I saw him picking up trash," said May.

When Gary trotted up ten minute later, he walked into a second scolding. This one was from Coach Hu.

Jack and Gary played on the same scrimmage team. Near the beginning of the game, Jack passed the ball to Gary. He ran into open space and called for a return pass, but Gary looked across the field and passed to Gretchen instead. Gretchen turned and passed to May. May lost the ball when she was challenged by a large boy. Even though it was only a scrimmage, Jack was frustrated. He had been in a perfect position to take a shot on goal, but Gary wouldn't pass the ball to him. The player Jack was supposed to be marking received the ball while Jack was fuming over Gary. Jack had to sprint hard to catch up and tackle him before he could shoot. This wasn't the first time Jack's speed had saved him from a big mistake.

Jack hoped that Coach Hu had noticed. Ms. Moreno was beside him, probably explaining about Gary.

For the rest of the scrimmage, Gary refused to pass to Jack. By the end of the game, Coach Hu had seen that Gary put his rivalry with Jack ahead of the team's interests. He took Gary aside for a talk. A few snatches of conversation floated on the breeze. Jack could make out ". . . good team pulls together. . . Keep this up and you'll be benched!" The coach broke off when the bus arrived.

Jack was excited when he jumped off the bus at home. He raced up the driveway, opened the door, and dashed in to tell Dad about the field trip.

The smell of dinner filled the house. Mom was cooking string beans and rice. She usually cooked more than one dish on one burner. The rice was steaming in a pot. Over the steaming rice she had put a steamer, and the string beans were in the steamer.

The fish was sizzling on the grill outside. Burning under the grill were the branches Mom had pruned from their apple trees. Dad had fixed a vent over the grill, and a filter to take the smoke out of the rising hot air.

Dad was pacing up and down in the kitchen. "I'm tired of hearing people gripe about the cost of gas and oil," he said. "Until the price goes up, people are not going to conserve. They're going to drive their gas-guzzling cars everywhere and waste energy at home. They're not going to look for clean sources of energy!"

"You got that right!" said Mom. She could listen to the same lecture over and over. She listened like it was the first time. Jack thought that was one reason Dad and Mom were so happy together.

While they were talking, Jack opened the refrigerator. He stood looking for a moment. "What have I told you?" asked Mom. "Decide what you want before you open the refrigerator, so you don't have to leave the door open long. You think something yummy will appear if you look long enough? If you don't know what we have, ask me." Jack sighed and closed the door.

At least Jack had his parent's attention now. "We talked about the energy shortage in science today. Ms. Moreno asked about our ideas for solving it."

"What were some of the suggestions?" asked Mom.

Jack told her. Mom listened and nodded as though she had never heard them before. "I also suggested that we have the school bus take us to school activities like games and practices. I said we should use the school bus to take us to games away from town."

"Great suggestion!" said Dad. "In fact, the college has just finished making an experimental bus. It runs on hydrogen. We haven't decided how to try it out. Maybe I should lend it to the school."

"That'd be great!" said Jack. "There's something else, too." He handed Dad the note from Ms. Moreno.

"Listen to this," Dad said to Mom. "Jack's science teacher wants to bring the class to our house for a field trip. They're supposed to learn all about how we make and use hydrogen. I have a great idea. I'll have the hydrogen bus pick them up at school and bring them here."

"That IS a great idea!" said Mom.

"The school board meets tonight," said Dad. "I'm going to go there and offer to lend them the hydrogen bus! Will dinner be ready soon?"

"It's ready now. If you eat quickly you'll have time to get to the meeting," said Mom.

A few hours later Dad came home from the meeting. His shoulders were slumped. "Do you want the bad news first or the good news?"

"Let's get the bad news over with. It's all over your face," said Mom.

"The school board turned down the hydrogen bus."

"I don't understand that," Mom said.

"The Schmidts opposed it. They give a lot of money to the town and the school. Nobody wants to offend them."

"I could get tired of them!" said Mom.

"What's the good news?" said Jack.

"The town decided to put bike paths along all the roads. One of your teachers proposed the idea Jack. She said that her class had suggested the idea. Now people can safely shop, go to school, and go to work on their bikes. Schmidt said he'd pay for the paths."

"That's generous," said Mom.

"That's not all he's paying for. Schmidt said the school bus is old and it doesn't get many miles to the gallon. He said he'd buy a new school bus and give the school a discount on gas."

"That's better than using the old bus," said Mom. "But not as good as a hydrogen bus."

"I'm still going to use the hydrogen bus for the field trip," said Dad.

On Wednesday, Jack's science class lined up single file. In the distance, a green speck moved down the road that led to the school. As it neared, Jack could make out the front of a bus. It grew larger until he could make out the word hydrogen on the bus.

The bus pulled up and stopped, but the driver did not turn off the engine. Dad jumped out of the bus. He opened the hood to show the engine to the class.

Everyone rushed up to look at the engine except Gary and his friends. They watched, hearing comments such as "Awesome!" and "Way cool!"

Looking bored, Gary strolled closer. Bit by bit, he edged closer until he was standing next to the engine. At first his expression was bored. Jack could tell he wasn't really bored, though. Every time Dad described a part of the engine, Gary's eyes fastened on that part. When Dad described a process, Gary's eyes darted back and forth between the parts used in the process. Pretty soon he wasn't even trying to look bored.

Dad finished and asked, "Any questions?"

The boy standing next to Gary started to raise his hand. Gary grabbed his hand and pulled it down.

Dad slammed the hood shut. Gary walked around to the back of the bus. He sniffed the air. "That's right," Dad

said. "It doesn't smell like the back of the school bus. That's because hydrogen doesn't make any pollution."

Gary scowled and looked at the ground. When the kids climbed into the bus, Gary took a seat by himself in the back. A couple of his friends came to sit near him. "If you sit near me, keep your mouth shut!" said Gary.

As they rode, Gary listened intently. Sometimes he would cock his head or cup his ear. Jack figured he was probably listening to the engine run. When the bus left the flatland and headed uphill, the sound of the engine changed a little. Gary nodded to himself.

The bus pulled up in front of Jack's house. The kids piled out. Dad showed them the house. "How are the north and the south wall of the house different?" he asked.

Gretchen said, "You have more windows on the south side. They are bigger too."

"That's so we can use the sun's energy during the winter," said Jack. "We planted trees in front of all these windows. In the summer, they're full of leaves and they shade the windows." The kids looked at the red, gold, and orange trees. "In a few weeks their leaves will be on the ground. Then they'll let the sunlight in."

Gary stood with his arms crossed. He kept his eyes on the sky.

"Tell them about the eaves, Jack." said Dad.

"Okay," said Jack, and he pointed to the roof. "These are a special length and they hang at a special angle. They're built so that in the summer, when the sun is high, the eaves shade the windows. Then in the winter, when the sun is lower, the sun's rays can come through the window. You can do the same thing with awnings."

Gary started to hum softly. Ms. Moreno silenced him with a fierce look.

Dad opened the front door and took them through the rooms along the south wall. "These dark tile floors absorb the sun's heat during the day. At night they give off the heat and help keep the house warm."

"During the summer we keep the windows closed during the day when it's hot. At night we leave the drapes open. We open the windows to let the cool air in. Then in the morning we close the windows. We don't use much air-conditioning."

Gary kept his eyes on the ceiling. He pretended to yawn when Ms. Moreno's back was turned.

"Our house is really well insulated," said Jack. "We don't lose much heat during the winter. During the summer the heat doesn't come in from outside."

"We could use some of Dr. Nelson's ideas at school," said Ms. Moreno. "We could plant trees near the windows. We could also put up awnings. I think it would be a good idea for the school rooms to have blinds. That way we could close them after school, and keep the heat in. I'm going to suggest that to the school board."

"Now let's look at our energy supply," said Dad.

Dad led the class outside to a small building. It had shiny black solar panels on the roof. The blades of a wind machine turned at the top of a pole. The pole was attached to the roof of the building

Gary walked around the building. He studied the solar panels and the spinning blades of the wind machine.

"We make all our hydrogen from water," explained Dad. "We use a process called electrolysis. This machine is called an electrolyzer. The electrolyzer needs electricity to run. We make electricity using solar power and wind power. Most days we have either sun or wind."

In spite of himself, Gary was standing as close as possible to the electrolyzer. He was watching it work.

Jack pointed to the electrolyzer. "Water enters the

electrolyzer. The machine then separates the water into hydrogen and oxygen. The hydrogen is collected. Then we use it as fuel."

"We burn some of the hydrogen directly. We use it to power the stove, refrigerator, lights, heaters, washer, and dryer," said Dad. "The rest of it we store in fuel cells."

"My dad writes articles for a camping magazine," said May. "When he camps, he uses a stove with a fuel cell."

"That's interesting," said Dad. "His stove is probably like some of our appliances."

Gary was interested. He examined the fuel cells closely.

"I wish you could get the whole town using some of your energy-saving ideas, Dr. Nelson," said Ms. Moreno.

"I know some traffic lights are solar powered, for example. You could probably also get people using hydrogen for some of their energy."

"I've been trying for years," said Dad. "People just don't take my research seriously."

"Well, I think they should take it seriously. We need to educate them. Do you think you could get the university to put on an energy workshop for the people in town?" said Ms. Moreno. "Once people really understand the issues and see how conservation and new forms of energy can help, we may be able to change their minds. We have a town meeting form of government, so everybody votes. You have to get a majority of the people on your side."

"A workshop is a good idea," said Dad.

"Meanwhile, the class and I will be writing up a proposal to take to the **selectmen**," said Mrs. Moreno. "We'll have to decide in class what it should be. When we decide, will you help us write it, Dr. Nelson?"

"You bet!" said Dad.

"Good. When we take it to the selectmen, we can ask them to call a town meeting."

On the ride back to school, Gary was silent. He listened to the engine all the way.

----

selectmen – People who are elected to office. Mainly in New England towns

CHAPTER 4

The Town Climbs Aboard

The night of the energy workshop, the town hall was packed. Almost every adult in town had come, and many of the kids seemed to be there.

Jack saw Mr. Schmidt walk in. "Dad!" he tugged at his father's sleeve and nodded toward Schmidt.

Dad walked to the back of the room and held out his hand to Schmidt. Jack was close behind.

"I'm glad you came," said Dad, as they shook hands.

Schmidt looked down, then up at Dad. "Gary told me I should come," he said gruffly.

First, Carlos's mom gave a talk about how to save heating oil and electricity. Her mouth tightened when somebody in the audience yelled, "You mean when we can GET electricity!" Even so, she continued, speaking about a few electric plants that used hydrogen as fuel. "Now Dr. Nelson will tell us more about hydrogen."

Dad described how hydrogen could power appliances. Then Dad introduced another scientist. He talked about hydrogen fuel cells that were made in sunny places, such as the desert. They could be ordered to power appliances. He described a project in the California desert. A small town had a fleet of minibuses powered by hydrogen. They provided transportation for the people in town. Hydrogen was made from water at a station. The hydrogen buses fueled at that station.

"Where can we get hydrogen heaters and hydrogen fuel cells?" asked a woman.

Jack's mom waved some catalogs and lists of suppliers. She passed them out. In them, people could find things that were powered by the sun, wind, or fuel cells.

One man stood up. "If we had some hydrogen buses, or any kind of buses, we wouldn't have to drive so much."

At first Schmidt sat in the back of the room, his arms crossed. Every so often his eyes rolled. When they started talking about the station where the fleet of hydrogen buses fueled, he began to look more interested. He then asked the question "Do we have the renewable resources in this town to set up a hydrogen station?"

"Yes," said Dad. "You can use the sun, the wind, and the river running through town."

Schmidt changed the subject, "You know, you get much better gas mileage if you have the right amount of air in your tires. If you've tried to ride a bicycle with soft tires, you will have noticed it takes a lot more energy to peddle than if you have hard tires. I invite you to bring your cars by the gas station. We'll check and inflate your tires for free."

"You don't have any gas!" shouted a man.

Schmidt turned red, but he continued. "You can save a lot of gas by driving the right way. I'll write up a list of tips about how to save gas while driving. You can pick them up at the station."

"Thanks," said Dad. "Those tips will be helpful." Mr. Schmidt nodded and sat down.

Another man stood up. "Are there any hydrogen buses anywhere near here?"

"The college has one hydrogen bus. We're looking for ways to test it for public use. The college is also partnered with a company that wants to make and sell hydrogen buses in the future. They may also be looking for a test site for their buses."

Jack watched his classmates leave the workshop. He could hear their excited chatter.

That wasn't all he heard though. Carlos's mother said to her husband, "You win! We'll move to San Francisco! I'm sick of being blamed for the blackouts!" Carlos followed them out, his shoulders slumped.

The next day, Jack's parents visited the science class. Ms. Moreno introduced them. "Dr. and Mrs. Nelson have some news," she said.

Dad told them the college wanted to set up a demonstration hydrogen project. Some businesses that made appliances powered by hydrogen fuel cells would donate a few heaters and other appliances to people like Mrs. Chin.

The college was also working with a company that would lend buses for the project. They would find a way to make hydrogen for the buses.

"It would be exciting if they chose our town," said Gretchen. "If people had buses, they wouldn't have to drive so much."

"Maybe we could have people call when they need to go somewhere," said Carlos. "Then the bus could pick them up. It would be like those shuttles some towns have."

"If we can get the school to accept the hydrogen bus the college offered, it can be used to give people rides when school is in session," said Mom.

"Let's write a plan and send it to the selectmen," said Ms. Moreno. She told students new to Vermont, that all voters voted at town meetings. They also elected selectmen, who ran the town between meetings. Selectmen could call special town meetings. They could ask the selectmen to call a special meeting about their plan.

"Let's brainstorm some ideas," said Ms. Moreno. As students suggested ideas, she listed them on the board.

At the end of the next day the plan was ready. The class had recommended bike paths beside the roads, hydrogen bus service, and some demonstration hydrogen appliances. They listed some energy-saving tips for businesses and town offices.

Jack, Mom, and Dad took it to the selectmen after school. The selectmen took the report. They promised to read it in a few weeks, but did not look interested.

The next day, Jack shivered in the chill morning air. The bus was 30 minutes late.

"Jack!" Mom was walking down the drive. "I saw you out here and called the school. The line has been busy for five minutes. Dad's going to drive you."

At 9:00, Dad arrived at school. He climbed out of the car and marched toward the office, Jack at his heels. The secretary was on the phone. Ms Stein, the principal, was on another phone. Coach Hu was helping out on another phone. As soon as Ms. Stein hung up, the phone started ringing again. She ignored the ring and explained to Dad, "All of Schmidt's stations are out of gas, Dr. Nelson. Even school buses can't get gas."

"The college is only a few miles away," said Dad.

"Shall I call and ask them to send over the hydrogen bus?"

"That would be wonderful!" said Ms. Stein. "I'll try to contact the students and tell them the bus is coming."

Dad said to Jack. "I'm going to City Hall. I want to post a notice on the website. People who are out of gas and need rides can call the bus between 10:30 and 2:00. While kids are in school the bus can give other people rides."

"Will you be driving the bus?" asked Jack.

"No, I'm going to the medical center to see if any of the doctors and nurses need rides to work. Then they can call patients who have appointments today. If a patient is out of gas, I'll drive them to the doctor."

"Why don't you stop by Schmidt's?" said Jack. "People who are out of gas will come to the station. He can tell them about the bus."

"Great idea!" said Dad.

That night Jack waited up for his dad. "What a day!" said Dad, rubbing his eyes. "The bus and my van were going nonstop. Oh!" His head jerked up. "Almost forgot! Schmidt had a truck with a full tank of gas. He delivered prescriptions from the drug store."

When Jack rolled out of bed the next morning, his dad had already left. At 8:00, the hydrogen bus picked Jack up. The kids had named it "Big Green."

After school, the regular, smelly yellow school bus pulled up. "Smellow Yellow!" cried the kids. The driver got out and announced, "Schmidt has gas!" The kids and teachers cheered wildly. "I miss Big Green, though," said Gretchen. Other kids nodded, holding their noses.

That evening, Dad burst through the door. His eyes blazed with victory! "Running out of gas got the selectmen's attention. They read our plan right away, and they've called a special town meeting!"

The next day, everyone at school was buzzing about the town meeting. Carlos couldn't get excited though. Jack kept thinking about how much he liked Carlos. Who would be his best friend after Carlos moved? Jack cheered up when Gary said, "I'm excited about the future of

energy and all these new machines are cool. I hope our parents won't hang on to the past." Jack thought that Gary was really referring to his own dad.

Ms. Moreno asked permission for the class to attend the town meeting. It was short for a town meeting. Nobody opposed the plan the class had submitted. After running out of gas, voters were ready for solutions.

When it came time to mark secret ballots, Schmidt took a long time. He sat staring at his ballot. Gary walked up to him and whispered in his ear. His father looked back, nodded, and marked his ballot. When he saw Jack watching, Gary raised his hand, thumb up.

After the ballot count a selectman announced that the proposal was approved. Nobody was surprised.

On Saturday morning, most of the business owners in town toured Jack's house. They made notes about energy saving ideas.

The business owners agreed to make changes. The car dealer would order some fuel efficient cars. The appliance store would look for more ENERGY STAR® appliances. Some wanted to carry at least a few hydrogen appliances. They looked through some catalogs and on the Internet.

Just as the last business owner left, the phone rang. It was Carlos. "We're not moving after all! Mom persuaded the electric company to set up a second power plant using hydrogen as a fuel. She's excited about it and she wants to run the plant. My dad thinks it is a good opportunity for mom so he wants to stay too."

For Jack, that was the best news of all. If the team could only win their first out of town soccer game that afternoon it would be a perfect day.

Jack hummed as he raked fallen leaves. The trees in front of the windows were now bare. The sun's rays slanted through the windows, hitting the dark tiles.

At 2:00, the kids waited for Big Green to take them to the game. When it arrived, they all piled in. Dad drove some of the parents in his minivan.

Jack rode with his stomach in knots. They would be playing against a very good team. He just hoped his team could play better.

When he stepped off the bus, Jack spotted his parents in the bleachers. Then he saw the Schmidts walking through the bleachers. To his surprise, Mr. Schmidt took a seat next to Dad. They began talking and nodding.

The team played well. All members played their best and the team worked well together. Unfortunately, the other team also played well. With the game almost over, the teams were level in a one to one tie. Jack's team needed one last big effort.

Gretchen was in the center of the field with the ball. Moving up the field, Jack called for the ball. Gretchen passed to Jack, and he trapped the ball. He dribbled up the sideline looking for a clear shot. Under pressure, he was unable to pass the ball anywhere but back to Carlos. Carlos tried to find an open teammate, but lost the ball to the other side. Jack, Gretchen, and Gary all had to sprint back to cover the goal. Jack got there first and intercepted a pass. Jack passed the ball to Gary and then moved into space. Gary saw Jack and quickly passed the ball to him. Jack collected the ball and raced up the field. He crossed the ball to Gretchen, who trapped it and took a shot. The ball flew into the top of the goal.

"Way to go!" Jack's team cheered. They had been working on this sequence for weeks. It had finally won them a game.

After the game, the players cheered, hugged, and jumped up and down. When they stopped and looked around, Jack saw his parents and Gary's standing on the field. They shook hands with every player. Then the two families walked off the field together.

"Mr. Schmidt says he'll build a hydrogen facility at one of his stations," said Dad. "The buses and city cars can get fuel there."

"Dad! That's great!" said Gary.

Schmidt put his arm around his son. "Well, we figured that if our sons could work together to win a soccer game, we can work together to win the energy game."

"Can I ask a favor, Dr. Nelson?" said Gary. "Will you teach me how a hydrogen powered engine works?"

"I think I can do better than that. I have a proposition for your dad," said Jack's father. He looked at Schmidt. "You were planning to buy a new bus for the school to replace Smellow Yellow. Instead, suppose I show you and Gary how to convert Smellow Yellow to run on hydrogen. Rather than pay for a new bus that runs on gasoline, you can pay to convert Smellow Yellow. It will cost you less than buying a new bus."

Gary looked at his dad. His eyes danced with excitement. His dad looked back at him, then smiled and looked up. "Deal!" he said.

"Yes!" shouted Gary. He was practically jumping for joy.

"But first things first!" said Schmidt. "Here's the pizzas I ordered for the team."

Mr. Schmidt began taking pizza boxes and cases of drinks out of the truck. The smell of hot crust, garlic, and tangy tomato sauce drifted in the air. Jack's mouth watered and his stomach rumbled.

"Who wants pizza?" Mr. Schmidt hollered. The team crowded round. Mom helped Mr. Schmidt pass out pizza slices and drink cans.

Gretchen bit into a slice. "This pizza is almost perfect. It only needs one thing."

"What's that?" asked Jack.

"A hydrogen truck to deliver it."

Everyone laughed. People had laughed about hydrogen before, but it was different now. This time Jack was laughing too.

Alternative Energies

Energy sources that will not run out are called renewable. Scientists are working to perfect systems that deliver and use renewable energy sources.

These energy sources could change daily life. Gasoline pumps might one day be history. Cars fueled by hydrogen would create less pollution.

Hydrogen is only one renewable energy source. Others may be more familiar to you. Solar power is energy gathered and stored from the sun. Wind is a source of energy too. Rotating blades that are pushed by wind create energy. Moving water is a common source of energy.

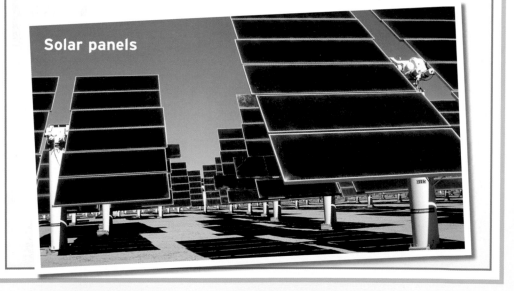

Solar panels

Hydrogen for Energy

Hydrogen can be used as a source of energy. It can be burned to produce heat. Hydrogen can be used to create electricity. Sometimes it does this in a special device called a fuel cell. Fuel cells can be used to power machines such as cars and buses. Hydrogen is the most plentiful element in nature. It is one of the elements that make up water. Scientists use technology to extract or take hydrogen from water.

Using hydrogen is good for the environment. Hydrogen does not produce a lot of pollution like oil, natural gas and coal does. The only thing left over after using hydrogen for energy is water.

Conserving Energy

Finding new energy sources is one way to make sure we have energy in the future. Another way is to use less energy. This is called conserving energy. If we use less energy we create less pollution. Using less energy will help keep the air and water safe for living things.

There are many ways to save energy. People can use public buses and trains instead of cars. This will lower the number of cars on the road. Building footpaths and bike paths may encourage people not to use their cars.

People can also help save energy at home. Household appliances that run on small amounts of energy are called efficient. Buying energy-efficient products can save energy. The ENERGY STAR® label on an appliance means it is very efficient.

Create an Energy Plan

Look around your school. Are there ways it could be more energy efficient? Write an energy plan for your school. List ways that the school could conserve energy and save money.

- Make a list of energy-saving ideas that were talked about in the story.

- Use the library or the internet to find out how people can conserve energy? Add the new information you find to your list.

- Make an energy plan for your school. Be sure to list small steps the school and students can take along with bigger ideas.

Read More About Energy Sources

Find and read more books about how people try to solve the energy problem. As you read, think about these questions. They will help you understand more about the topic.

- What are some sources of energy?

- What are the benefits of these types of energy?

- What are the problems with these types of energy?

- How can people create energy while protecting the planet?

SUGGESTED READING
Reading Expeditions
Science Issues Today:
Using Energy

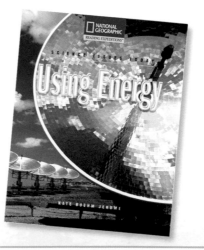